A book for all ages...

Get Back Up and Keep on Trying

by Holly Roberts Merrell

Illustrations by Galih Winduadi

Copyright © 2019 by Holly Roberts Merrell
Illustrations: Galih Winduadi

All rights reserved. No part of this book may be reproduced by any mechanical, photographic, or electronic process, or in the form of a phonographic recording; nor may it be stored in a retrieval system, transmitted, or otherwise be copied for public or private use--other than for "fair use" as brief quotations embodied in articles and reviews without prior written permission of the publisher. The intent of the author is only to offer information of a general nature to help you in your quest for emotional and spiritual well-being. In the event you use any of the information in this book for yourself, the author assumes no responsibility for your actions.

Library of Congress Control Number: 2020902177

ISBN: 978-1-951982-02-7
Digital ISBN: 978-1-951982-03-4

This is a book for all ages....

There are lessons in this book that we can all learn from no matter our age, our gender, our race, or our religion. Do you ever feel like you're a failure, and can't seem to succeed at anything you do? Do you find that "fear" or even the "fear of pain" often governs you and the choices you make? We are meant to have joy in this life. Lots of it! But so often we let fear rob us of all the wonderful experiences that life has to offer. Often times we stay in our comfort zones and don't push ourselves to do hard things. We end up taking the easy way out. But I'll tell you from experience, there is not much growth, confidence, or joy found in taking the easy way out. We discredit ourselves and our abilities. We limit ourselves by taking this road. We are so much more than we give ourselves credit for, and we can do so much more than we allow ourselves to do. As you read through this book, think of all the times that you let an opportunity pass you by because of that little voice in our head that says..."that's too scary," "that's too hard," or "what if I get hurt?" So often we let this fear get in the way of all those things, that deep down inside, we really want to do, but yet we make up excuses for why we can't do them. The more we challenge ourselves by getting out of our comfort zones and stretching beyond what limits we have set for ourselves, we will gain confidence, mental toughness and happiness that we didn't have before. As you read this book remember this...."knowledge isn't power until it's applied." This is not just a cute little book with rhyming words. Rather it is a book with a lesson. The power is in the application. The power comes from putting the things you learn into action. So when you feel that you have failed, or didn't do as good as you had hoped, take the advice from this book and get back up and keep on trying!

You've never failed, until you've quit!

Life will knock you down.
It's not about "if" but "when."
It's just part of this life;
it will happen again and again.

But don't look at it as a bad thing;
It's actually part of the plan.
It will happen to every person
whether you're a child, a woman or man.

Some people see it as failure;
it defeats them and shuts them down.
But the only time you fail
is when you stay down on the ground.

Pick yourself up and keep going
no matter how hard the hit.
Because the only time you fail
is when you decide to quit.

It will take a little effort.
Sometimes it will take a lot.
At times it will take much more
than you feel like you have got.

But...
When you push yourself and keep going
and you push with all your might,
you'll find that you can do it.
What you want is within sight.

Something I'm not proud of,
but I'll share it anyway,
is an experience that I went through,
and learned a harder way.

There was a time that I played basketball,
and I thought I knew the game;
but someone told me I was doing it wrong,
and then I felt ashamed.

Instead of asking them to explain it
and teach me a little more,
I let my pride get in the way.
I quit playing and shut that door.

But I loved the sport so much,
that I gave it another shot.
But I threw in the towel again;
I didn't like the way my coach taught.

You see, I didn't like to be yelled at,
And my coach did that a lot.
I was afraid of getting yelled at
if I didn't make my shot.

What I didn't realize then,
but obviously now I do,
is that coaches yell and they get mad;
it's just something you have to go through.

If you want to play a sport
you've got to listen to your coach;
toughen up your feelings
and take a different approach.

Don't give up because he's mad
or saying you're doing it wrong;
just listen to his instructions,
then keep going and be strong.

If you decide to give up,
you'll have to live with that regret,
and I'll tell you from experience
it's not easy to just forget.

It's really hard to let it go,
and I wish I could change the past.
In that moment I chose to quit,
I didn't realize how long it'd last.

So….. think again before you quit;
you've got to keep on climbing.
When things get tough, say to yourself,
"Push through it, keep on trying!"

Well..... what if I didn't fall,
rather I took the easy way out?
Is this the same as quitting,
or is this a whole new route?

Ask yourself, when no one's watching
and you are all alone,
do you take the easy way out,
thinking "no one will ever know?"

Or do you push yourself to be better,
and give it all you've got?
Or do just barely enough
and hope you don't get caught?

There are times when we fall;
we need to get up and keep trying.
There are also times to push ourselves,
because inside, it's satisfying.

It builds our confidence,
and it makes us feel good.
We find we can do things,
we never knew that we could.

Sometimes we don't push ourselves
because of this thing called fear.
We let it take over
and allow it to steer.

We let it take control
of what we do and what we say.
Instead of deciding ourselves,
we let fear get in the way.

We may think to ourselves,
"what if that" or "what if this,"
but when we let fear fill our thoughts
there is so much we will miss.

We may fear that we will fail,
or we may be afraid of pain,
but if we let fear control us
there is nothing we will gain.

We can't go around
afraid that we may fail,
because when opportunities come,
we won't try, and we'll just bail.

Nothing good comes from giving up;
no confidence is gained.
The confidence we did have,
is now a little drained.

If you're afraid of pain,
which a lot of times we are,
it will hold you back from trying,
and you really won't get far.

Pain is only temporary;
it may last a minute or a day.
It may even last a lot longer,
it's really hard to say.

But when you push through pain
and tell yourself you can do it,
a part of you grows stronger
and it's easier to get through it.

Pain gets easier to handle;
it's not as scary anymore.
You come to find it's not as bad
as you thought it was before.

So when fear and pain get in your way
and prevent you from wanting to try,
take control, don't let them win.
Don't let opportunities pass you by.

When you have to do something scary
and it seems quite terrifying,
you may fall, but you've not failed;
get back up and keep on trying.

When someone pushes you down
and it hurts and you are crying,
you've got to tell yourself
to get back up and keep on trying.

When you fall hard and feel the pain
and it feels quite horrifying,
just remember you can do it;
get back up and keep on trying.

Because when you try and end up falling,
or not doing as good as you'd like,
if you try again and again,
you'll eventually win that fight.

You've never failed until you quit;
you've actually succeeded.
You've given more than you thought you had;
your expectations you've exceeded.

The things you'll learn and the places you'll go
when you tell yourself you can,
you'll be amazed at how much you've grown
since the day that you began.

So what is something you're dealing with?
Do you have a coach who is mean?
Do you want to stop drinking soda?
Are you addicted to caffeine?

Do you want to try and snowboard
but you're afraid that you'll get hurt?
Do you want to ride a dirt bike
but you're scared of crashing in the dirt?

What if you're an artist,
or at least you like to draw.
Has someone put you down
and said your drawings are "blah"?

Would you like to ride a horse
but you're afraid you'll get bucked off?
Well, you're right, it may happen,
just don't land in the horse's trough!

You'll never know till you're on that horse
exactly what will happen.
You might fall off, you might stay on,
you might be crying or a laughin'.

But if you avoid these things
and let fear get in the way,
you won't have very much growth
at the end of every day.

Life is about growing
and learning new things,
it's through these experiences,
that we grow our wings.

Our confidence grows,
and we feel like we can soar,
simply because,
we don't quit anymore.

So, if you are afraid
to try something new,
or if someone ends up saying,
"that's something you can't do."

Accept it as a challenge
and prove that you can do it.
It may take a lot of effort,
but keep going, you'll get through it.

Sometimes your greatest teachers
are the ones that say you can't,
but this is when you decide
which seed you're going to plant.

Can you? Or can't you?
You get to choose.
You get to decide
whether you win or you lose.

Get back up and
keep on trying!

Books by Holly Roberts Merrell...

To learn more about the author and more in depth detail of her personal experiences regarding her books, please visit hollyrobertsmerrell.com.

www.ingramcontent.com/pod-product-compliance
Lightning Source LLC
Chambersburg PA
CBHW041818040426

42452CB00001B/13